Irish Whiskey
Tasting Journal

"Always carry a flagon of whiskey in case of snake bite. Furthermore, always carry a small snake"
— **W.C. Fields**

Irish Whiskey Styles

Single Malt
- Made with 100% Malted barley at a single distillery
- Distilled in Copper Pot Stills
- Typically distilled three times, but may only be twice
- Matured in used barrels, typically Bourbon, but may also be Sherry, Port, Madeira, etc.

Single Grain
- Uses raw grains such as corn or wheat
- While not a primary ingredient, a small amount of raw barley may be used
- Distilled in Column Stills
- A typically lighter spirit, which receives much influence for the casks
- Matured in used barrels, typically Bourbon, but may also be Sherry, Port, Madeira, etc.

Single Pot Still / Pure Pot Still / Pot Still
- Includes both malted and unmalted barley in the Mash Bill
- The unmalted barley gives the whiskey a unique, spicy flavor profile
- Minimum of 30% unmalted, 30% malted, other grains not to exceed 5%
- Distilled entirely in Copper Pot Stills
- Typically distilled three times, but not required
- Matured in used barrels, typically Bourbon, but may also be Sherry, Port, Madeira, etc.

Blended
- Any combination of fully distilled Single Grain, Single Malt, and/or Single Pot Still
- Frequently uses larger base of grain whiskey
- Combines the lighter, sweeter taste of grain, with the more aggressive or flavorful Single Malt or Single Pot Still
- Accounts for over 90% of both Irish and Scotch Whiskeys

Date: _____

Place: _____

Whiskey name: _____

Whiskey style: _____

Nose:

_____

_____

_____

Palate:

_____

_____

_____

Finish:

_____

_____

_____

Notes/Thoughts/Impressions:

_____

_____

_____

Date: _____

Place: _____

Whiskey name: _____

Whiskey style: _____

Nose:

_____

_____

_____

Palate:

_____

_____

_____

Finish:

_____

_____

_____

Notes/Thoughts/Impressions:

_____

_____

_____

Date: _____

Place: _____

Whiskey name: _____

Whiskey style: _____

Nose:

_____

_____

_____

Palate:

_____

_____

_____

Finish:

_____

_____

_____

Notes/Thoughts/Impressions:

_____

_____

_____

Date: _____

Place: _____

Whiskey name: _____

Whiskey style: _____

Nose:

_____

_____

_____

Palate:

_____

_____

_____

Finish:

_____

_____

_____

Notes/Thoughts/Impressions:

_____

_____

_____

Date: _____

Place: _____

Whiskey name: _____

Whiskey style: _____

Nose:

_____

_____

_____

Palate:

_____

_____

_____

Finish:

_____

_____

_____

Notes/Thoughts/Impressions:

_____

_____

_____

Date: _____

Place: _____

Whiskey name: _____

Whiskey style: _____

Nose:

_____

_____

_____

Palate:

_____

_____

_____

Finish:

_____

_____

_____

Notes/Thoughts/Impressions:

_____

_____

_____

Date: _____

Place: _____

Whiskey name: _____

Whiskey style: _____

Nose:

_____

_____

_____

Palate:

_____

_____

_____

Finish:

_____

_____

_____

Notes/Thoughts/Impressions:

_____

_____

_____

Date: _____

Place: _____

Whiskey name: _____

Whiskey style: _____

Nose:

_____

_____

_____

Palate:

_____

_____

_____

Finish:

_____

_____

_____

Notes/Thoughts/Impressions:

_____

_____

_____

Date: _____

Place: _____

Whiskey name: _____

Whiskey style: _____

Nose:

_____

_____

_____

Palate:

_____

_____

_____

Finish:

_____

_____

_____

Notes/Thoughts/Impressions:

_____

_____

_____

Date: _____

Place: _____

Whiskey name: _____

Whiskey style: _____

Nose:

_____

_____

_____

Palate:

_____

_____

_____

Finish:

_____

_____

_____

Notes/Thoughts/Impressions:

_____

_____

_____

Date: _____

Place: _____

Whiskey name: _____

Whiskey style: _____

Nose:

_____

_____

_____

Palate:

_____

_____

_____

Finish:

_____

_____

_____

Notes/Thoughts/Impressions:

_____

_____

_____

Date: _____

Place: _____

Whiskey name: _____

Whiskey style: _____

Nose:

_____

_____

_____

Palate:

_____

_____

_____

Finish:

_____

_____

_____

Notes/Thoughts/Impressions:

_____

_____

_____

Date: _____

Place: _____

Whiskey name: _____

Whiskey style: _____

Nose:

_____

_____

_____

Palate:

_____

_____

_____

Finish:

_____

_____

_____

Notes/Thoughts/Impressions:

_____

_____

_____

Date: _____

Place: _____

Whiskey name: _____

Whiskey style: _____

Nose:

_____

_____

_____

Palate:

_____

_____

_____

Finish:

_____

_____

_____

Notes/Thoughts/Impressions:

_____

_____

_____

Date: _____

Place: _____

Whiskey name: _____

Whiskey style: _____

Nose:

_____

_____

_____

Palate:

_____

_____

_____

Finish:

_____

_____

_____

Notes/Thoughts/Impressions:

_____

_____

_____

Date: _____

Place: _____

Whiskey name: _____

Whiskey style: _____

Nose:

_____

_____

_____

Palate:

_____

_____

_____

Finish:

_____

_____

_____

Notes/Thoughts/Impressions:

_____

_____

_____

Date: _____

Place: _____

Whiskey name: _____

Whiskey style: _____

Nose:

_____

_____

_____

Palate:

_____

_____

_____

Finish:

_____

_____

_____

Notes/Thoughts/Impressions:

_____

_____

_____

Date: _____

Place: _____

Whiskey name: _____

Whiskey style: _____

Nose:

_____

_____

_____

Palate:

_____

_____

_____

Finish:

_____

_____

_____

Notes/Thoughts/Impressions:

_____

_____

_____

Date: _____

Place: _____

Whiskey name: _____

Whiskey style: _____

Nose:

_____

_____

_____

Palate:

_____

_____

_____

Finish:

_____

_____

_____

Notes/Thoughts/Impressions:

_____

_____

_____

Date: _____

Place: _____

Whiskey name: _____

Whiskey style: _____

Nose:

_____

_____

_____

Palate:

_____

_____

_____

Finish:

_____

_____

_____

Notes/Thoughts/Impressions:

_____

_____

_____

Date: _____

Place: _____

Whiskey name: _____

Whiskey style: _____

Nose:

_____

_____

_____

Palate:

_____

_____

_____

Finish:

_____

_____

_____

Notes/Thoughts/Impressions:

_____

_____

_____

Date: _____

Place: _____

Whiskey name: _____

Whiskey style: _____

Nose:

_____

_____

_____

Palate:

_____

_____

_____

Finish:

_____

_____

_____

Notes/Thoughts/Impressions:

_____

_____

_____

Date: _____

Place: _____

Whiskey name: _____

Whiskey style: _____

Nose:

_____

_____

_____

Palate:

_____

_____

_____

Finish:

_____

_____

_____

Notes/Thoughts/Impressions:

_____

_____

_____

Date: _____

Place: _____

Whiskey name: _____

Whiskey style: _____

Nose:

_____

_____

_____

Palate:

_____

_____

_____

Finish:

_____

_____

_____

Notes/Thoughts/Impressions:

_____

_____

_____

Date: _____

Place: _____

Whiskey name: _____

Whiskey style: _____

Nose:

_____

_____

_____

Palate:

_____

_____

_____

Finish:

_____

_____

_____

Notes/Thoughts/Impressions:

_____

_____

_____

Date: _____

Place: _____

Whiskey name: _____

Whiskey style: _____

Nose:

_____

_____

_____

Palate:

_____

_____

_____

Finish:

_____

_____

_____

Notes/Thoughts/Impressions:

_____

_____

_____

Date: _____

Place: _____

Whiskey name: _____

Whiskey style: _____

Nose:

_____

_____

_____

Palate:

_____

_____

_____

Finish:

_____

_____

_____

Notes/Thoughts/Impressions:

_____

_____

_____

Date: _____

Place: _____

Whiskey name: _____

Whiskey style: _____

Nose:

_____

_____

_____

Palate:

_____

_____

_____

Finish:

_____

_____

_____

Notes/Thoughts/Impressions:

_____

_____

_____

Date: _____

Place: _____

Whiskey name: _____

Whiskey style: _____

Nose:

_____

_____

_____

Palate:

_____

_____

_____

Finish:

_____

_____

_____

Notes/Thoughts/Impressions:

_____

_____

_____

Date: _____

Place: _____

Whiskey name: _____

Whiskey style: _____

Nose:

_____

_____

_____

Palate:

_____

_____

_____

Finish:

_____

_____

_____

Notes/Thoughts/Impressions:

_____

_____

_____

Date: _____

Place: _____

Whiskey name: _____

Whiskey style: _____

Nose:

_____

_____

_____

Palate:

_____

_____

_____

Finish:

_____

_____

_____

Notes/Thoughts/Impressions:

_____

_____

_____

Date: _____

Place: _____

Whiskey name: _____

Whiskey style: _____

Nose:

_____

_____

_____

Palate:

_____

_____

_____

Finish:

_____

_____

_____

Notes/Thoughts/Impressions:

_____

_____

_____

Date: _____

Place: _____

Whiskey name: _____

Whiskey style: _____

Nose:

_____

_____

_____

Palate:

_____

_____

_____

Finish:

_____

_____

_____

Notes/Thoughts/Impressions:

_____

_____

_____

Date: _____

Place: _____

Whiskey name: _____

Whiskey style: _____

Nose:

_____

_____

_____

Palate:

_____

_____

_____

Finish:

_____

_____

_____

Notes/Thoughts/Impressions:

_____

_____

_____

Date: _____

Place: _____

Whiskey name: _____

Whiskey style: _____

Nose:

_____

_____

_____

Palate:

_____

_____

_____

Finish:

_____

_____

_____

Notes/Thoughts/Impressions:

_____

_____

_____

Date: _____

Place: _____

Whiskey name: _____

Whiskey style: _____

Nose:

_____

_____

_____

Palate:

_____

_____

_____

Finish:

_____

_____

_____

Notes/Thoughts/Impressions:

_____

_____

_____

Date: _____

Place: _____

Whiskey name: _____

Whiskey style: _____

Nose:

_____

_____

_____

Palate:

_____

_____

_____

Finish:

_____

_____

_____

Notes/Thoughts/Impressions:

_____

_____

_____

Date: _____

Place: _____

Whiskey name: _____

Whiskey style: _____

Nose:

_____

_____

_____

Palate:

_____

_____

_____

Finish:

_____

_____

_____

Notes/Thoughts/Impressions:

_____

_____

_____

Date: _____

Place: _____

Whiskey name: _____

Whiskey style: _____

Nose:

_____

_____

_____

Palate:

_____

_____

_____

Finish:

_____

_____

_____

Notes/Thoughts/Impressions:

_____

_____

_____

Date: _____

Place: _____

Whiskey name: _____

Whiskey style: _____

Nose:

_____

_____

_____

Palate:

_____

_____

_____

Finish:

_____

_____

_____

Notes/Thoughts/Impressions:

_____

_____

_____

Date: _____

Place: _____

Whiskey name: _____

Whiskey style: _____

Nose:

_____

_____

_____

Palate:

_____

_____

_____

Finish:

_____

_____

_____

Notes/Thoughts/Impressions:

_____

_____

_____

Date: _____

Place: _____

Whiskey name: _____

Whiskey style: _____

Nose:

_____

_____

_____

Palate:

_____

_____

_____

Finish:

_____

_____

_____

Notes/Thoughts/Impressions:

_____

_____

_____

Date: _____

Place: _____

Whiskey name: _____

Whiskey style: _____

Nose:

_____

_____

_____

Palate:

_____

_____

_____

Finish:

_____

_____

_____

Notes/Thoughts/Impressions:

_____

_____

_____

Date: _____

Place: _____

Whiskey name: _____

Whiskey style: _____

Nose:

_____

_____

_____

Palate:

_____

_____

_____

Finish:

_____

_____

_____

Notes/Thoughts/Impressions:

_____

_____

_____

Date: _____

Place: _____

Whiskey name: _____

Whiskey style: _____

Nose:

_____

_____

_____

Palate:

_____

_____

_____

Finish:

_____

_____

_____

Notes/Thoughts/Impressions:

_____

_____

_____

Date: _____

Place: _____

Whiskey name: _____

Whiskey style: _____

Nose:

_____

_____

_____

Palate:

_____

_____

_____

Finish:

_____

_____

_____

Notes/Thoughts/Impressions:

_____

_____

_____

Date: _____

Place: _____

Whiskey name: _____

Whiskey style: _____

Nose:

_____

_____

_____

Palate:

_____

_____

_____

Finish:

_____

_____

_____

Notes/Thoughts/Impressions:

_____

_____

_____

Date: _____

Place: _____

Whiskey name: _____

Whiskey style: _____

Nose:

_____

_____

_____

Palate:

_____

_____

_____

Finish:

_____

_____

_____

Notes/Thoughts/Impressions:

_____

_____

_____

Flying Piggy Publishing hopes you enjoyed this journal.

Scan the code above to visit us at **www.flyingpigg.us/books**
to find more journals, logs, devotionals, etc.

As always, please enjoy your whiskey responsibly.
Please don't drink and drive.

Made in the
USA
Middletown, DE